Awesome Facts
about

Tidal Waves

This edition published in 2001
© Aladdin Books Ltd 1999
Produced by
Aladdin Books Ltd
28 Percy Street
London W1P 0LD

ISBN 0-7496-4245-9 (paperback)
Previously published in hardcover
in the series "I Didn't Know That"
ISBN 0-7496-3424-3 (hardback)

First published in Great Britain in 1999 by
Aladdin Books/Watts Books
96 Leonard Street
London EC2A 4XD

Editor: Liz White
Design: David West Children's Books
Designer: Flick Killerby
Illustrators: Peter Roberts – Allied Artists,
Jo Moore

Printed in the U.A.E.

Awesome Facts
about
Tidal Waves

Kate Petty

Aladdin / Watts
London • Sydney

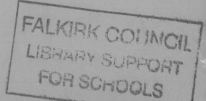

Contents

Introduction

Did *you* know that most tidal waves are started by earthquakes? ... that the Moon moves water? ... that the correct name for a tidal wave is a tsunami? ... that the sea can light up a town?

Discover for yourself amazing facts about tidal waves: how they start, the power they generate – and the havoc they can cause.

Look out for this symbol which means there is a fun project for you to try.

Is it true or is it false? Watch for this symbol and try to answer the question before reading on for the answer.

Wild waves

Tidal waves are powerful enough to wash away whole cities. A 16-metre-high tidal wave swamped the people of Lisbon, Portugal, as they fled from falling, burning buildings in the earthquake of 1755, which killed 60,000 people.

When an underwater earthquake cracks the seabed, huge pressure pushes the water above into waves. At sea the waves are far apart, but they get closer and higher as they reach the shore.

The ancient Greek philosopher Plato described a perfect city called Atlantis that disappeared under the Mediterranean Sea. It might have been engulfed by a tidal wave, or it might have simply slipped into the sea.

! The biggest tidal wave ever was 85 m, taller than a skyscraper.

Fire and water

Volcanoes can set off *tsunamis*. When Krakatoa in Indonesia blew its top in 1883 the explosion was heard 5,000 km away. The volcano caused tsunamis that killed 37,000 people on the nearby islands of Java and Sumatra.

 True or false?

There are more than 10,000 volcanoes under the Pacific Ocean.

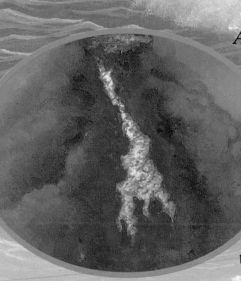

Answer: **True**
Part of the Pacific Ocean is called the 'ring of fire' because it has thousands of underwater volcanoes (left) and 90% of tsunamis occur here.

The eruption of Krakatoa in Indonesia could be heard in Australia.

'Tsunami' is the correct word for what we call tidal waves. It means 'harbour wave' in Japanese. These waves are set off by earthquakes and volcanoes.

Where plates pull apart, magma rises and forms an ocean ridge.

Volcanoes form where two ocean plates meet.

The Earth's *crust* is covered in *plates*. Where two ocean plates meet, one is forced down into the heat of the Earth's *mantle* and may melt into *magma*, which can erupt as a volcano.

The highest wave ever ridden was almost 20 m high.

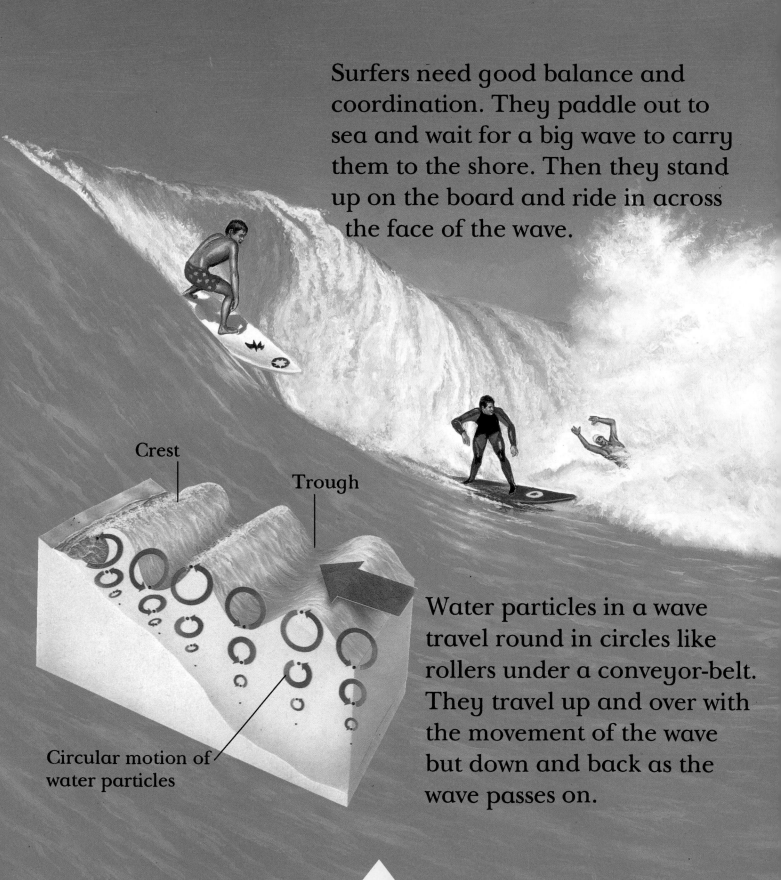

Surfers need good balance and coordination. They paddle out to sea and wait for a big wave to carry them to the shore. Then they stand up on the board and ride in across the face of the wave.

Crest

Trough

Water particles in a wave travel round in circles like rollers under a conveyor-belt. They travel up and over with the movement of the wave but down and back as the wave passes on.

Circular motion of water particles

Ocean motion

The sea stays still as the waves move forward. The water in a wave moves in circles. The wave is pushed forwards by the wind and the movement of the water within it, but the sea itself stays in the same place.

SEARCH & FIND & SEARCH & FIND & SEARCH

Can you find three surfers?

Strong winds blow for great distances over the open sea, causing *swells* that can travel for thousands of kilometres. The rough seas seem to appear from nowhere – 'out of the blue'.

In Mexico surfers can ride a wave for almost two kilometres.

Mooning around

The Moon causes tides from far out in space. Tides happen because the *gravity* of the Sun and the Moon pull on the Earth's oceans, causing the water to rise and fall as the world spins.

This coast road in Holland is built on land that was once under the sea. High *dikes* hold back the sea.

Extra high 'spring' tides happen when the Sun and the Moon are in line and both pulling in the same direction. Lower 'neap' tides happen when the Sun and Moon are pulling in different directions.

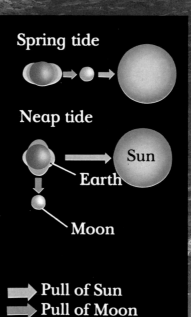

Spring tide

Neap tide

Sun

Earth

Moon

➡ Pull of Sun
➡ Pull of Moon

A Dutch story tells of a boy who plugged a hole in a dike with his finger.

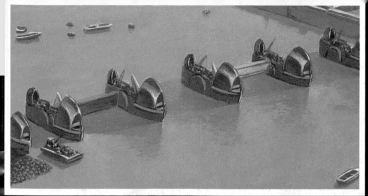

The River Thames is affected by the tides. The Thames Barrier at Woolwich (left) was built to protect London from flooding during exceptionally high tides.

SEARCH & FIND & FIND & SEARCH & FIND

Can you find four lit houses?

Ship smashers

Tropical storms at sea can strike suddenly. They can soon whip up mountainous waves. Old wooden ships stood little chance, but even modern boats can be wrecked in stormy seas.

One of the most dangerous places in the world is Cape Horn at the very tip of South America. Sailors have always feared the dangerous conditions and the icy waters there.

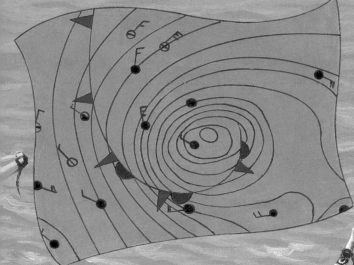

A ship's computerised weather maps predict stormy weather which occurs when a warm front (round symbols) meets a cold front (triangles).

 Lighthouses warn sailors away from rocky shores at night. Make your own lighthouse from a cardboard tube. Cut out windows and paint it with stripes. Stand a torch inside and pop a cardboard lid on top. Complete the scene with a papier mâché rock and plasticine boats.

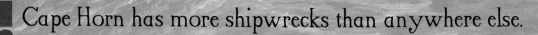
Cape Horn has more shipwrecks than anywhere else.

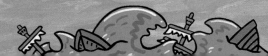

Storm surges

Storms at sea can come ashore. Huge waves whipped up by a hurricane at sea can hit the land ahead of the storm itself. Ships end up stranded hundreds of metres from the coastline.

——— Hurricane

Storm surge

When huge waves come ashore ahead of the storm it is called a storm surge.

A storm surge can raise the level of the sea by six metres. Flooding after a tropical storm in Bangladesh in 1991 killed 250,000 people and left millions without their homes, animals or possessions.

Home wreckers

People who live on the coast are most at risk from tsunamis. In 1992, two thousand villagers were killed when a tsunami, 26 metres high, crashed on to their fragile, wooden homes in Flores, Indonesia, causing devastation.

 True or false?
People at sea don't notice tsunamis.

Answer: **True**
In 1896 Japanese fishermen had no idea that one of the waves beneath their boats went on to kill 27,000 people back home.

In 1998, islanders settling down for the evening in Papua New Guinea were caught off-guard by three 15-metre tsunamis, set off by an earthquake 20 km out to sea. More than 2,000 people died. These survivors came back to find their homes had been wrecked.

In 1960, a tsunami in Chile killed over 1,000 people and destroyed 50,000 homes. 14 hours later it slammed into Hilo, Hawaii, killing a further 61 people.

Alaska

Hawaii

Isla de Chiloe
Chile

The Scotch Cap lighthouse in Alaska was wiped out by a tsunami in 1946.

Helicopters are useful in sea rescues because they can hover while a survivor is winched to safety. They use radar and infra-red scanners to pinpoint people in the sea.

True or false?
Sailors have been known to survive for several days after capsizing in cold waters.

Answer: **True**

In January 1997 round-the-world yachtsman Tony Bullimore spent five days under his upturned 18-metre yacht before being rescued 1,300 sea miles south of Australia.

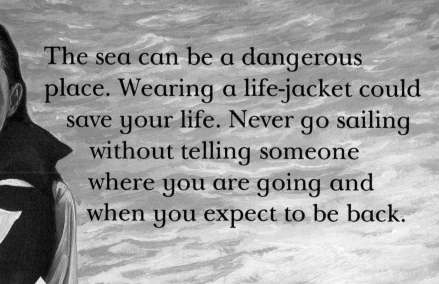

The sea can be a dangerous place. Wearing a life-jacket could save your life. Never go sailing without telling someone where you are going and when you expect to be back.

Utterly unsinkable

Some boats are specially designed to stay afloat whatever the weather. Modern lifeboats have the power to skim over the tops of very high waves. They are also designed to right themselves if they keel over. Satellite links help them to locate a ship in trouble.

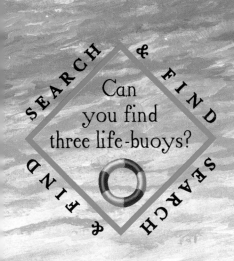

SEARCH & FIND & SEARCH & FIND

Can you find three life-buoys?

! Two fishermen were adrift for 177 days after a cyclone hit.

Families who live in tsunami areas need an *evacuation* plan and an emergency kit on hand. The kit should contain: a torch and extra batteries, a portable battery radio, a first-aid kit with medicines, emergency food and water, a tin-opener, money and sturdy shoes.

Eye-witnesses to tsunamis describe the way the sea first pulls back with a hissing, sucking sound, rather like the noise of a jet engine, before it rears up in a huge, engulfing wave. The rumble of a nearby earthquake is another warning sign.

! Tsunamis can be caused by meteorites landing in the sea.

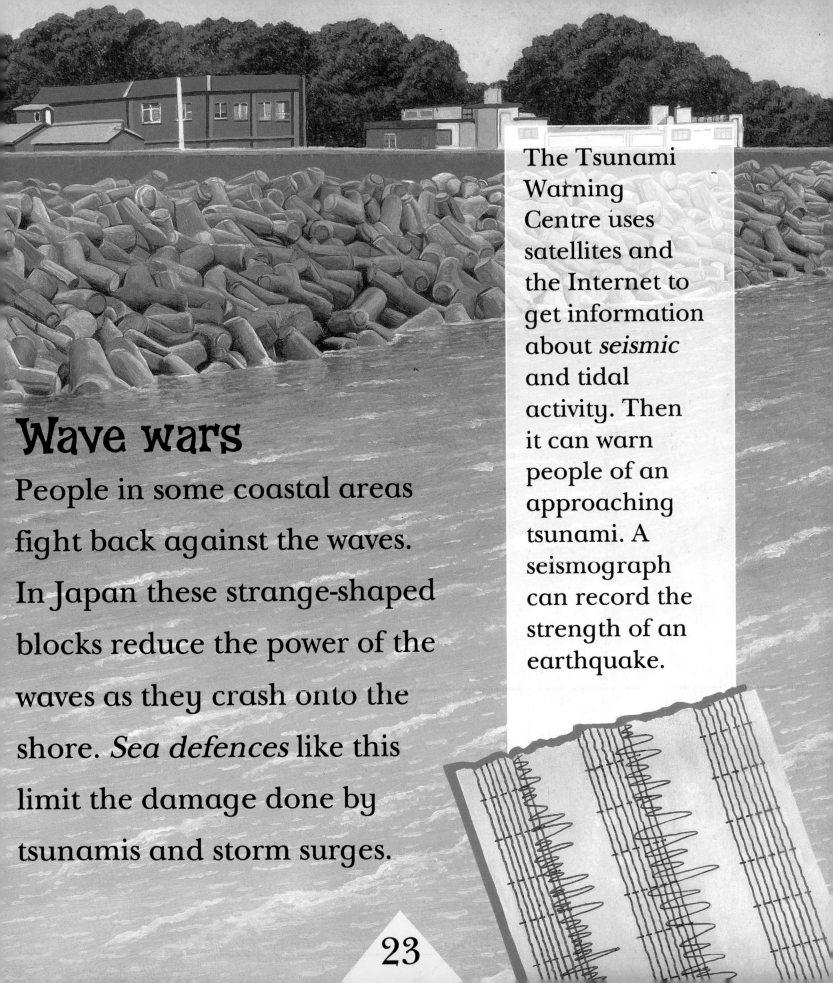

Wave wars

People in some coastal areas fight back against the waves. In Japan these strange-shaped blocks reduce the power of the waves as they crash onto the shore. *Sea defences* like this limit the damage done by tsunamis and storm surges.

The Tsunami Warning Centre uses satellites and the Internet to get information about *seismic* and tidal activity. Then it can warn people of an approaching tsunami. A seismograph can record the strength of an earthquake.

'St. Elmo's fire' can sometimes be seen around the mast of a ship in stormy seas. It happens when the moving air inside a storm cloud builds up static electricity which gathers around the highest point of the ship, the mast.

Waterspouts are an awe-inspiring sight but fortunately they are rarely dangerous. They usually last about 15 minutes. Most waterspouts are only 5-10 m thick and between 50-100 m high.

Water twisters

Sometimes ocean storms create incredible weather. A waterspout is a *tornado* at sea. When rapidly rising warm air meets falling cool air it sets up a spinning funnel which sucks up the water from the surface of the sea.

 True or false?
Sometimes one waterspout can follow after another.

Answer: **True**
At Martha's Vineyard, USA, (off the coast, north of New York) in 1896, there were three waterspouts within just 45 minutes.

 In 1958, sailors in the Adriatic saw five waterspouts at once.

In 1944, the five bombers of Flight 19 disappeared without trace into the 'Devil's Triangle' (also called the Bermuda Triangle). Despite many rational explanations, people still believe there is something spooky about the sea here.

Mysteries of the sea

Unpredictable weather may be the cause of many sea mysteries. Over 70 ships and 20 planes have been lost in the 'Bermuda Triangle', maybe because this stormy area of the Atlantic Ocean has undersea earthquakes and volcanoes as well as awkward *currents*.

True or false?

El Niño can cause flooding in the desert.

Answer: **True**
In 1983, El Niño brought high winds and flooding to the Arizona desert. It can cause strange weather like snow in places that are usually hot or drought in wet places. It can also often bring violent weather.

'El Niño' is the movement of warm water in the Pacific, eastwards from Indonesia towards the Americas.

America

Warm water

❗ El Niño can cause flowers to bloom in the desert.

Wave power

People can harness sea energy for use on land. Using the power of waves and tides is not a new idea. However, there are experimental systems now, that have shown that they can provide large amounts of electricity.

The Osprey 2000 wave system can operate near the shore.

Run a tap on to a toy water wheel and see how the power of the water turns the wheel. The turning of the wheel produces energy. You can make a water wheel with a cotton reel that can spin on a pencil.

Wave power is a way of generating electricity. One day it should be possible to harness the power of strong, deep water waves out at sea.

The biggest water power plant is Itaipu. Built by Brazil and Paraguay, it supplies a quarter of Brazil's electricity and over three quarters of Paraguay's.

Tide-powered water mills have been used for thousands of years.

Glossary

Crust
The hard, rocky outer layer of the Earth's surface.

Currents
Movement of water in the oceans set up by the winds, water temperatures and the spin of the world.

Dike
A wall that holds back water.

Evacuation
Clearing people from a dangerous building or place.

Gravity
A force that 'pulls' objects towards each other like an apple falling to the Earth.

Magma
The layer of molten rock beneath the Earth's surface (part of the mantle).

Mantle
The hot layer of the Earth between the crust and the core.

Plates

The Earth's crust is divided into about 15 plates that are always moving on the liquid surface of the magma below.

Sea defences

Any way of protecting land from the power of the sea.

Seismic

To do with earthquakes (seism is another word for earthquake).

Swell

The rise and fall of the waves on the open sea.

Tornado

A spinning storm on land, also called a 'twister'.

Tropical storm

Violent storms, with high-speed winds, that form over tropical seas in very warm weather. Called hurricanes, typhoons or cyclones depending on where they are.

Tsunami

Giant wave caused by an earthquake or volcano, a better word for 'tidal wave'.

Index